DO IT YOURSELF

Composting

Decomposition

Buffy Silverman

Heinemann
LIBRARY

www.heinemann.co.uk/library

Visit our website to find out more information about Heinemann Library books.

To order:

☎ Phone 44 (0) 1865 888066

▤ Send a fax to 44 (0) 1865 314091

▭ Visit the Heinemann bookshop at **www.heinemann.co.uk/library** to browse our catalogue and order online.

Heinemann Library is an imprint of **Pearson Education Limited**, a company incorporated in England and Wales having its registered office at Edinburgh Gate, Harlow, Essex, CM20 2JE – Registered company number: 00872828

Heinemann is a registered trademark of Pearson Education Limited.

Text © Pearson Education Limited 2008
First published in paperback in 2008
The moral rights of the proprietor have been asserted.

Edited by Louise Galpine and Kate DeVilliers
Designed by Richard Parker and Tinstar Design Ltd, www.tinstar.co.uk
Illustrations Oxford designers and illustrators
Picture research by Hannah Taylor
Production: Victoria Fitzgerald

Originated by Chroma Graphics (Overseas) Pte. Ltd
Printed and bound in China by Leo Paper Group.

ISBN 978 0 431 111 22 3 (hardback)
12 11 10 09 08
10 9 8 7 6 5 4 3 2 1

ISBN 978 0 431 111 38 4 (paperback)
12 11 10 09 08
10 9 8 7 6 5 4 3 2 1

British Library Cataloguing in Publication Data
Silverman, Buffy
Composting : decomposition. - (Do it yourself)
631.8′75

A full catalogue record for this book is available from the British Library.

Acknowledgements
The publishers would like to thank the following for permission to reproduce photographs: ©Alamy pp. **31** (Mark Boulton), **43** (Jeff Smith); ©Corbis pp. **5** (Brand X/Alison Miksch), **15** (Design Pics), **28** (Clouds Hill Imaging Ltd), **29** (Clouds Hill Imaging Ltd); ©DK Images pp. **21** (Peter Anderson), **35** (Clive Streeter), **37** (Peter Anderson); ©FLPA (Derek Middleton) p. **39**; ©Masterfile (Anders Hald) p. **33**; ©Photolibrary pp. **4** (Oxford Scientific), **9** (Phototake Science), **11** (Oxford Scientific), **13** (Oxford Scientific), **17** (Garden Picture Library), **41** (Garden Picture Library); ©Science Photo Library pp. **8** (Micheal P. Gadomski), **12** (Sinclair Stammers), **19** (Jerry Mason).

Cover photograph of a woman with red wiggler earthworms, used in composting, reproduced with permission of ©Corbis (Macduff Everton).

The publishers would like to thank Nick Lapthorn for his help in the preparation of this book.

Every effort has been made to contact copyright holders of any material reproduced in this book. Any omissions will be rectified in subsequent printings if notice is given to the publishers.

Disclaimer
All the Internet addresses (URLs) given in this book were valid at the time of going to press. However, due to the dynamic nature of the Internet, some addresses may have changed, or sites may have changed or ceased to exist since publication. While the author and publishers regret any inconvenience this may cause readers, no responsibility for any such changes can be accepted by either the author or the publishers. It is recommended that adults supervise children on the Internet.

Contents

Any words appearing in the text in bold, **like this**, are explained in the glossary.

What is composting?

Leaves, branches, and trees are always changing in a forest. Leaves fall from the trees and cover the ground. Twigs and branches fall to the forest floor, too. As the wind blows, more dead branches and leaves tumble down. As trees die, they also fall to the forest floor.

No one comes to the forest to pick up the fallen leaves, branches, and trees. Why don't the leaves from the trees pile higher and higher on the forest floor? What happens to broken branches and tree trunks?

When leaves and branches fall to the ground, they start to **decay**. Insects chew up dead leaves, breaking them into smaller and smaller pieces. Worms eat bits of leaves as they crawl through the soil. Microscopic **bacteria** break them down even further.

Decomposers break leaves down and mix them into soil.

Nature's recyclers

Worms, insects, bacteria, and other living things that break down dead plants and animals are called **decomposers**. Decomposers are nature's **recyclers**. They break down dead plants and animals, which become part of the soil. Decomposers add chemicals called **nutrients** to the soil. Plants take in nutrients with their roots and use them to grow.

Just as leaves and branches break down in a forest, they can break down in your garden, too. People **compost** garden waste and food scraps. Composting is the process of turning garden and food waste into a rich **fertilizer** called compost.

Anyone can turn garden and food scraps into compost.

A compost pile is a place where decomposers live. There, the decomposers get plenty of air, water, and food. They break down food and garden waste and quickly turn it into compost that can be mixed with soil.

When people compost, they turn waste into something useful. Instead of food scraps ending up in the rubbish, they become rich compost that can be added to a garden. The compost makes the soil richer and helps plants to grow.

Flowing energy

Decomposers are part of every **habitat**. Without them the world would be buried beneath layers and layers of dead plants and animals. Decomposers recycle dead plants and animals, which become part of **fertile** soil. Like all living things, decomposers need **energy** to live and grow. That energy comes from their food.

All energy on Earth starts with the Sun. Green plants use the Sun's energy to make food inside their leaves. Green plants are called **producers**. They make their own food and use the energy in it to grow. Animals get energy from plants. Some animals eat other animals that have eaten plants. Animals are called **consumers** because they eat other living things.

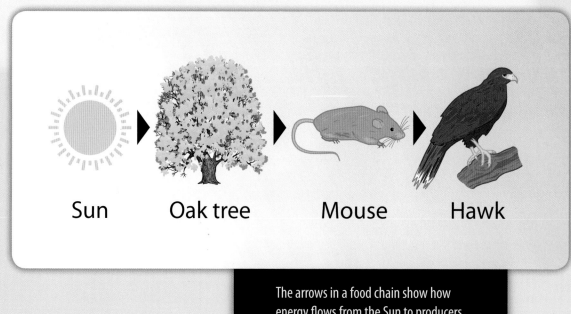

| Sun | Oak tree | Mouse | Hawk |

The arrows in a food chain show how energy flows from the Sun to producers, consumers, and decomposers.

Food chains

In a **food chain**, plants, animals, and decomposers are linked together. A food chain shows the path of energy.

For example, an oak tree starts one food chain. The tree uses the Sun's energy to make food and grow. A mouse may eat acorns from the oak. It gets energy from the tree. A hawk may catch and eat the mouse, and it then gets energy from the mouse. When the plants and animals in the chain die, decomposers return the nutrients in the dead plants and animals to the soil.

Build your food chain!

You need a lot of energy to grow, learn, and play. Your energy comes from the foods you eat. Choose three foods that you eat. Draw a food chain that shows how energy flows from your food to you. Include producers, consumers, and decomposers in your chain.

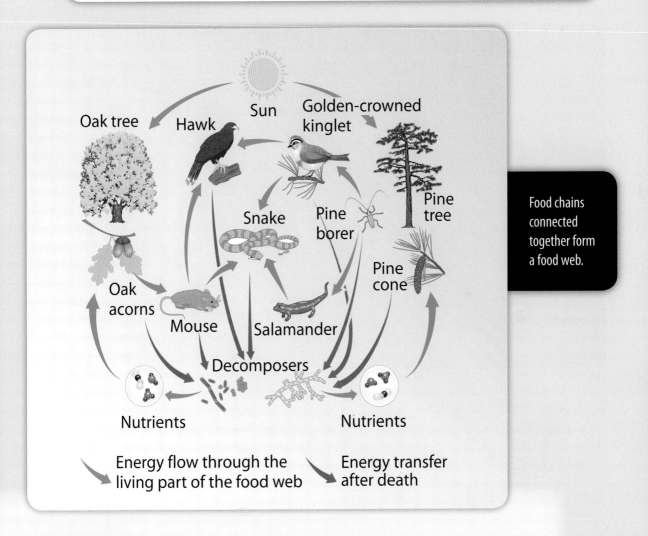

Oak tree

Hawk

Sun

Golden-crowned kinglet

Pine tree

Snake

Pine borer

Pine cone

Oak acorns

Mouse

Salamander

Decomposers

Nutrients

Nutrients

Energy flow through the living part of the food web

Energy transfer after death

Food chains connected together form a food web.

Food webs

Living communities are complicated. Animals often eat many different foods. A hawk that eats a mouse also eats songbirds that eat insects. Many chains linked together form a **food web**. Decomposers break down all plants and animals. New plants then use the nutrients that decomposers add to soil.

Meet the decomposers

Soil has many layers, starting with the dead bugs, leaves, twigs, and grasses that are scattered on top. Parts of feathers, bones, and larger animal bodies may be there, too. These dead plants and animals store **nutrients** and **energy**.

Fungi growing on a dead log decay it.

Scavengers at work

Crows, foxes, and other animals eat pieces of dead animals that they find. Animals that eat dead animals are called scavengers. They feed on the dead animals, leaving behind smaller pieces that other **decomposers** can eat. Beetles and flies also swarm over dead animals and chew them into tiny pieces.

Other beetles and millipedes chew up dead leaves and branches. Their chewing breaks plants into smaller and smaller pieces. Earthworms eat bits of leaves as they tunnel through the soil. The worms break leaves down further and mix them into the soil.

Mushrooms grow in damp soil. Mushrooms are a kind of **fungi**. Like all fungi, they cannot make their own food. Instead they get nutrients from dead leaves, logs, and animals that they grow on. As they do so, they **decay** the dead plants and animals.

Millions and millions

Bacteria are too small to see without a microscope. Millions and millions of them grow on dead plants and animals. They grow quickly and make more and more bacteria. Because there are so many bacteria, they are able to use all the **matter** left in dead plants and animals.

When decomposers break down matter, they release nutrients that were in the bodies of the plants and animals. These nutrients end up in the soil and can be taken up by plants. Decomposers **recycle** the nutrients, so they can be used over and over again.

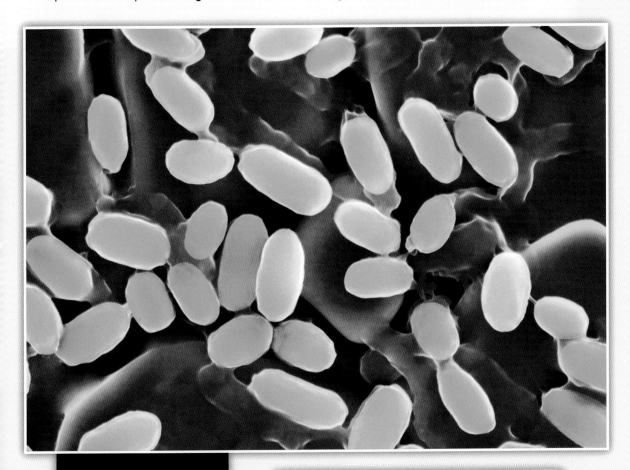

Millions and millions of microscopic bacteria consume dead plants and animals.

Decomposers underfoot

There are more decomposers living in a spoonful of topsoil than there are people on Earth!

Mould garden

For this experiment you will need:

* Two pieces of bread
* A plant mister with water
* Two plastic zip-top bags
* A marker

 1 Choose fresh bread without preservatives. (Preservatives are chemicals that stop **mould** from growing.) Spray the bread lightly with water to make it slightly damp. Set one piece of bread on a counter for 30 minutes. Place the other piece on soil outside for 30 minutes.

2 Using a marker, label one plastic bag "inside mould" and the other "soil mould". Put each piece of bread in the correct bag and seal it carefully.

3 Put both bags in a cupboard or other dark place.

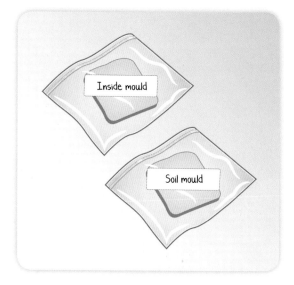

4 After three days, check your bags for mould growth. Once you see mould growing, do not open the bags, as many people are allergic to moulds. Record the size and colour of the mould you see.

5 Continue observing the bread for the next four days. Record your observations. Draw a picture of each piece of bread at the end of one week.

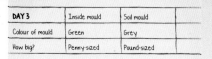

DAY 3	Inside mould	Soil mould	
Colour of mould	Green	Grey	
How big?	Penny-sized	Pound-sized	

How moulds work

Decomposers are all around, even if they are not visible to the naked eye. Microscopic mould **spores** float in the air. When they land on something that has nutrients, the spores start to grow into mould.

Moulds are a type of fungus. A mushroom is another type of fungus, which may grow on a fallen log. A mushroom is a **fruiting body**. Fruiting bodies make spores.

Spores float through the air and grow into new fungi. If you dig underneath a mushroom in the soil, you will find the body of a fungus. It looks like a mass of white threads growing in all directions.

This mass of threads breaks down whatever it grows upon. Special chemicals ooze out of a fungus. The chemicals break down the fungus's food, so it can absorb the nutrients. In bread, nutrients **dissolve** into water, and a fungus takes them in.

Spores from the air land on bread and grow into a thick bread mould.

Decomposers in action

Look up at a towering tree. The tree is home to an entire community of animals, which may include squirrels, caterpillars, or birds. Like all other trees, one day a healthy tree will die and become part of the soil.

Even before a dying tree falls, **decomposers** start to weaken it. Beetles burrow under bark and tunnel through wood. Woodpeckers drill into the tree, searching for insects. They leave holes behind, where **bacteria** and **fungi** grow. The inside of the tree starts to rot, forming cavities (openings) where animals live.

> It can take 200 years or more for a dead tree to completely decay.

A tree falls

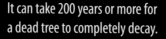

During a storm, the wind may topple a dead tree. Although the tree is dead, it soon swarms with new life. Beetles, ants, and termites creep under the bark and bore into wood. They make tunnels deep inside. Boring beetles have microscopic animals living in their guts that can **digest** tough wood. Bacteria and fungi soften the wood as they decompose it.

As the wood softens, more and more animals feed on it. Worms and mites crawl through tunnels. Centipedes race through and catch spiders and insects. Insects, spiders, and woodlice may lay their eggs in the damp log. Other animals come and eat up the eggs.

New plants grow

As it rots, the inside of a log acts like a sponge, soaking up water. A wet log is a perfect place for new plants to grow. Sprouting tree seeds send their roots down into the wet log. Moss grows on top of the log. Snails and slugs crawl on top, feeding on the moss.

The tree that once stood tall is now a **decaying** log, home to hundreds of thousands of creatures. The inside no longer looks like wood. It is filled with a jumble of holes. Some of it crumbles apart. Deep inside the log, it is brown and soft. The rotting tree is ready to become part of the soil.

Insects weaken a tree by feeding on it.

Steps to follow

1 Dig some soil from your garden and place it in a plastic container.

2 Moisten a paper towel and place it at the bottom of a glass jar.

3 Place the funnel inside the glass jar. Cover the smaller funnel opening with the wire mesh.

4 Scoop the soil onto the wire screen. Shine a desk lamp over the jar and turn off other lights.

5 After several hours, check to see what has crawled onto the paper towel. Record in a notebook how many and what kinds of animals you find.

6 Return the soil and animals to your garden.

What lives in soil?

For this experiment you will need:

* Garden soil
* A plastic container
* Paper towels
* A glass jar
* A funnel
* A small piece of wire mesh
* A desk lamp
* A notebook

14

Other types of soil

Collect another soil sample from a different location – try the woods or a playground or a lawn. Repeat the activity. Do you find more or fewer animals than in the garden soil? Are there different kinds of animal in different soils?

Sandy soils with little decaying material have less food for animals. You might find more animals in garden soil than in a playground. Hard soils that have been walked on or rode over have little air. Soils that are good homes have food, water, and air.

On this cliff edge you can see different layers of soil that have formed over thousands of years.

Soil is made from rocks, dead plants, animals, water, and air. But if you took a jar and mixed all these things, you would not get soil. That is because it is missing an important ingredient: time. It takes thousands of years for water and wind to wear rocks into tiny particles that become part of soil. Decomposers need time to gradually return bits of dead **matter** to the soil.

Worm farm

In the natural world, **decomposers recycle** dead plants and animals, turning them into **fertile** soil. Decomposers release **nutrients** in dead animals and plants. Living plants that grow in fertile soil pick up nutrients through their roots and use them as they grow.

When people **compost**, they recycle food scraps and garden waste to make fertile soil. Composting reduces the amount of rubbish that a household makes, which would otherwise go to a **landfill**. Through composting you can turn rubbish into something useful for a garden or for growing plants in pots.

You might not have a garden or other place for an outdoor compost pile. Even so, you can still turn food scraps into **fertilizer** using a worm farm. If you dig in rich garden soil, you find worms tunneling through. They break down dead plants and return nutrients to the soil. Worms in a worm farm do the same thing.

Compost makers

In a worm farm, worms tunnel through newspaper or other shredded material. When food scraps are added, the worms eat them, turning scraps into compost as they pass through their bodies. Because the worms are fed vegetable and fruit scraps with plenty of nutrients, the compost is an excellent fertilizer.

You can set up a worm farm inside or outside your home. During the cold winter months, worm farmers bring their bins inside and make compost all year. Your teacher might let you set up a worm farm at school as a class project, or your parents might let you set one up at home. A worm farm does not take up much space.

A worm farm is easy to set up and does not smell bad. All you need is a bin, some strips of newspaper, food scraps, and worms.

Life of a worm

Worms in a worm farm live for about a year. They will **reproduce** in the worm farm, so it always has new worms.

Worms will eat bread crusts, salad leaves, and orange peel.

Worm biology

In all, there are about 1,800 different kinds of earthworm that live in soils all over the world. Some worms are so tiny that they cannot be seen without a microscope. Others grow to more than 1 metre (3 feet) in length. But most common earthworms are about as long as your finger.

The segments of a worm look like rings around its body.

Esophagus
Crop
Gizzard
Male reproductive organs
Female reproductive organs
Hearts
Intestine
Mouth
Clitellum
Anus
Segment

A worm's body

Although there are many kinds of earthworm, most share the same body plan. Earthworms have 100 or more **segments**. Inside each segment are muscles, **nerves**, and **blood vessels**. A worm has five hearts to pump its blood from one end to the other.

When a worm crawls, it uses muscles and **bristles**. Each segment has muscles that go around the worm's body in a circle. A worm also has long muscles running the length of its body. First, a worm squeezes its circular muscles, pushing its front end forward. Then, it squeezes its long muscles, bringing its rear end toward the front. On the outside of each worm segment are four pairs of bristles. The bristles grip the earth, helping a worm to slow down or stop.

Hungry worms

As a worm crawls, it eats its way through soil. A worm's mouth is on its first segment. A flap of skin covers the small mouth. A worm's **anus** is at the last segment. The worm swallows pieces of dead plants and animals that are in the soil. It also eats **bacteria**, **fungi**, and other microscopic creatures. As **matter** goes through a worm, the worm grinds everything up. Matter that the worm cannot **digest** leaves its body. This matter, called worm **casts**, is a rich fertilizer that helps plants grow.

Millions of worms

If you dug up all the earthworms living under a football field, you would find about five million of them.

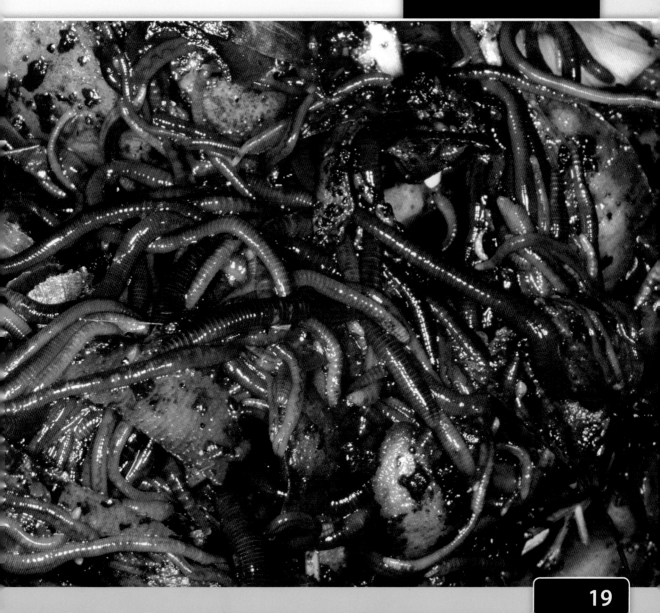

Red worms are the best kind of worm for a worm farm.

Setting up a worm farm

For this activity you will need:

* A plastic bin
* A drill
* Newspaper
* Four blocks
* A tray

1 Choose a plastic bin where your worms will live. The container should be about 60 cm (24 inches) long, 45 cm (18 inches) wide, and 29 cm (8 inches) high. Find a lid or sheet of dark plastic for a cover.

2 Ask an adult to drill eight holes about 0.5 cm (1/4 inch) wide in the bottom of the container, and four holes of the same size in each side.

3 Tear newspaper into strips about 1 to 3 cm (1/2 to 1 inch) wide and 30 to 60 cm (12 to 24 inches) long.

4 Moisten strips of newspaper. The newspaper should be about as damp as a wrung-out sponge. Fill the bin three-quarters full with the newspaper strips. Finally, gently mix this bedding material.

5 Set the bin on the blocks, placing the try underneath.

Warning: Adult supervision is required for this project.

Raising worms

To raise healthy worms, you must supply a home that is like the worms' natural **habitat**. In a shallow container, your worms will be able to tunnel close to the surface. The cover will keep the worm farm dark and moist, like the soil.

Worms need air to breathe. When worms tunnel through soil, they make spaces that fill with air. After you give the worms loose bedding material, they can tunnel through and make air spaces. This is called soil aeration. Fresh air flows into your worm farm through the holes.

Red worms (*Eisenia fetida*) live in the top 15 cm (6 inches) of outdoor soil.

Worms do not have lungs. Instead they breathe through their skin. A worm's skin must be damp for air to pass in and out. Oxygen is a gas in air that animals breathe. Oxygen **dissolves** in water and passes through the worm's skin and into its bloodstream. If there is too much water, a worm can drown, but any extra water that gets into your worm farm will drain out of the holes in the bottom.

Steps to follow

1 Buy red worms for your worm farm. Earthworms and other worms that you dig from your garden will not survive well in a worm farm. Many pet stores and fishing shops sell red worms. You can also order worms online. Red worms are the best kind of worm to use in a worm farm.

3 Place the worms on top of the bedding. Turn a light on near the bin. Worms do not like bright light and will burrow headfirst into the newspaper bedding to escape it.

2 Start with about 0.5 kg (1 pound) of worms. This amount of worms will eat about 1.6 kg (3.5 pounds) of food scraps each week.

4 Turn off the light as soon as most of the worms have burrowed. Sprinkle a handful of sand or soil into the bin.

5 Put your bin a cool, dark place so that your worms can adjust to their new home.

0.5 kg

Big worms and little worms

The number of worms in 0.5 kg (1 pound) depends on the age of the worms. About 150,000 newborn worms weigh 0.5 kg . If your worms are adults, there will be about 1,000 worms in 0.5 kg.

Living in a bin

Red worms adapt easily to living in a worm farm and will eat almost any kind of food scraps. They especially like soft food that has started to rot. They will also tunnel through the newspaper bedding and start to eat it if it is moist and soft. Sand or soil helps worms grind up their food inside their bodies.

Bookworms

Since paper is made from wood, the worms can decompose it. They can turn newspaper and other bedding into compost. Let them settle into their new home for a few days before you begin adding other food.

Moisture, air, food, darkness, and warm temperatures will all help your worms to thrive.

Caring for your worms

Steps to follow

Feeding your worms

For this activity you will need:

* Food scraps
* A scale to weigh food

1 Save food scraps in a plastic container in the refrigerator. Feed your worms raw fruits and vegetables, breads, grains, crushed eggshells, tea bags, and coffee grounds. Do not feed them meat, bones, oily foods, or cheese. While worms can eat these foods, the foods can attract mice and insect pests.

2 Cut or break up the food scraps into small pieces. Crush any eggshells. The smaller the pieces of food, the easier it is for your worms to eat them.

3 Measure the food. Feed your worms once a week, giving them 1.6 kg (3.5 pounds) of food for every 0.5 kg (1 pound) of worms.

4 Bury the food in the bedding. To do this, lift up the bedding and move it to the side. Add the food scraps. Cover the food with bedding. Bury the food in a different spot each week.

5 Fluff up the bedding with your hands. This will add air to the worm farm.

6 Cover the worms with the lid or sheet of plastic.

7 Wash your hands when you have finished.

From food to compost

A worm has no teeth. It sucks small bits of food into its mouth and softens the food with moisture from its body. The food travels from the worm's mouth to its **gizzard**. As it eats, grains of sand and soil get trapped in the gizzard. Muscles in the gizzard scrape sand against the food, grinding it up.

From the gizzard, the food travels to the worm's **intestine**, where it is **digested**. The **energy** from the food is absorbed by the blood and is pumped to all parts of the worm. Ground-up parts that a worm cannot digest come out its **anus**. That material is the worm's **casts** – the **compost** that your bin produces. In this way, worms **recycle** your food scraps.

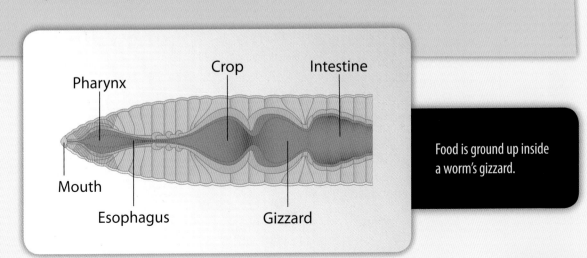

Pharynx · Crop · Intestine · Mouth · Esophagus · Gizzard

Food is ground up inside a worm's gizzard.

Favourite foods

For this activity you will need:

* Three types of food scraps
* A scale
* A notebook
* Three pieces of scrap paper
* Rubber gloves

1 You might notice that some of the foods that you give your worms disappear faster than other foods. Do your worms prefer some food scraps to others? Choose three different food scraps to compare. For example, you might choose carrots, bread, and apples.

2 Cut or break the foods into pieces of about the same size.

3 Weigh each food sample and feed the worms the same amount of each food. For example, you could begin with 0.2 kg (1/2 pound) of each type of food. Record the types of food, weight, and date when you begin your experiment.

4 Bury the foods in different parts of the worm farm. Remember that the bedding will be partially eaten and look more like compost now. Put the carrot pieces in one corner, the bread pieces in another corner, and the apple pieces in another corner.

5 After three days, uncover the foods. Wearing rubber gloves, separate the foods from the bedding and collect each type of food. Place each sample on a piece of scrap paper.

6 Compare the size of the food piles that remain. If possible, weigh each pile of food. Calculate how much of each type of food your worms have eaten. Which food did your worms prefer?

Food	Weight at start	Weight after one week
Apple	0.2 kg	
Carrot	0.2 kg	
Bread	0.2 kg	

A worm menu

Your worms probably like moist foods better than dry foods. They probably prefer soft foods to hard foods.

In nature worms eat dead plants and animals that are partly rotten. The **bacteria** and **moulds** that begin to **decay matter** soften it and make it moist. When worms eat decaying matter, they also consume bacteria and moulds.

What size is best?

You could also experiment to see what size food particles the worms eat the fastest. Repeat the food choice experiment. However, instead of giving the worms different types of food, give them food pieces of three or four different sizes.

Worm families

While you are feeding your worms and mixing the bedding, you might find worm **cocoons**. Worm cocoons are smaller than a grain of rice and shaped like tiny yellow lemons. Inside the cocoons, baby worms are growing and will soon hatch in your farm.

Have you ever wondered if your worms are male or female? They are both! Worms are **hermaphrodites**. Each worm has both male and female parts in its body.

An adult worm has a **clitellum**, a swollen area near its head-end. When worms **reproduce**, they join their clitella and exchange **sperm**. Both worms in a pair make eggs that are **fertilized** during mating. Inside the clitellum, cocoons are made. After a week or two, the worms shed their cocoons. Each cocoon usually has one to five baby worms inside. In two or three weeks, the babies hatch from the cocoon.

Baby worms grow inside a cocoon.

Worm babies

Young worms look like thin, white pieces of thread. They are only about 1.25 cm (half an inch) long. But baby worms grow fast as they tunnel through the worm farm. They live on their own as soon as they hatch, eating their way through the bedding. The first worm to hatch from a cocoon may eat the other babies in the cocoon.

After a couple of weeks, tiny worms crawl out of a cocoon.

In about 60 days, the worms grow a clitellum. Then they are adults. They are ready to reproduce and make new cocoons.

Search your worm farm for all stages of a red worm's life cycle. Can you find cocoons? The cocoons darken from yellow to brown before they hatch. Also try to find growing worms and adults.

Population boom

Worms grow up and have babies quickly. An adult worm may lay one cocoon a week! The number of red worms in your bin can double or triple in a single year. More worms can eat more food and make more compost for you.

Monitoring your worm farm

New worms will be born in your worm farm, replacing old worms that die and decompose in the worm farm. Your bin can turn food waste into compost for a long, long time.

Follow these tips to keep your worm farm healthy:

1. Food: At the end of each week, check to see if the worms have eaten most of the food. If food disappears completely, try feeding them a little more. If there is a lot of food left over, feed them less and cut the food up into smaller pieces. If the worms do not eat one type of food, stop feeding it to them. Uneaten food attracts flies and causes unpleasant smells. Bury food to stop bad smells.

2. Moisture: Worms like damp places best. Check to see that the bedding is moist. Spray it with a mister and keep the bin covered so that it stays dark and damp. Too much water is not healthy for your worms. If water fills in all the spaces, there will not be enough air for the worms. Extra water drains out of the bin's holes, but if the bedding is soaking wet, add more newspaper strips and turn over the bedding. Leave the cover off to let water evaporate.

3. Temperature: Worms can survive in a wide range of temperatures, but will thrive best in a cool, dark bin. The ideal temperature of your bin is between 4° C (40° F) and 30° C (85° F). Use a thermometer to check the temperature of your worm farm. Keep the bin away from heaters and windows.

4. Bedding: Turn over the bedding each week to add air to your worm farm. If you notice smells and flies in your bin, add more newspaper strips. Feed less food until the smells disappear.

Worms in the cold

Earthworms burrow near the surface of the soil when it is warm and damp. When the temperature drops below freezing, earthworms burrow deep in the ground, where the soil stays warmer.

If you take good care of your worms, they will live for a year or more.

Compost from worms

Steps to follow

1 In a healthy worm farm, worms quickly turn food into **compost**. After three to five months, you will notice that there is mostly compost and little newspaper bedding in your bin. It is time to remove the compost the worms have made.

2 Before you harvest the compost, stop feeding your worms for two weeks. The worms will not die. They will be ready to move into fresh bedding if they are hungry.

3 Wear rubber gloves when handling the compost. Push the worms and their **casts** to one side of the bin. Take out any large pieces of food or newspaper that are not broken down.

4 Put fresh bedding on the empty side of the bin. Moisten the bedding. Begin feeding your worms again. Only bury food on the side of the bin with fresh bedding.

5 Cover the side of the bin with fresh bedding. Leave the other side exposed to light and allow it to dry out. The worms will crawl over to the side of the bin with new bedding. They prefer to be in the dark, damp side of the bin and will be hungry for new vegetable scraps.

6 After two to three weeks, almost all of the worms will be on the side of the bin with fresh bedding. Remove the compost from the open side of the bin. Replace it with fresh newspaper strips. Dampen the strips and begin to bury food on that side. Cover the entire bin. It is important to remove the casts every few months, because too many casts can harm the worms. To stay healthy, the worms need fresh bedding and food.

What next?

You can use the compost that you harvest for growing plants. When mixed with soil, worm casts make a great **fertilizer** that helps plants grow.

Rich brown compost is ready to be mixed into the soil to help plants grow.

Steps to follow

 1 Label four plant pots with tape, marking them A, B, C, and D.

 2 Fill each pot as follows: place 240 ml (1 cup) of potting soil in pot A. Mix 15 ml (1 tablespoon) of compost with 240 ml (1 cup) of potting soil in pot B. Mix 45 ml (3 tablespoons) of compost with 240 ml (1 cup) of soil in pot C. Put 120 ml (1/2 cup) of compost and 120 ml (1/2 cup) of soil in pot D.

 3 Plant two bean seeds in each pot. Push the seeds about 1.25 cm (1/2 inch) below the surface. Water each pot with an equal amount of water, about 60 ml (1/4 cup).

 4 Place all four pots on a sunny windowsill.

 5 Continue to water the pots at the same time, with an equal amount of water every few days. The soil should feel damp.

Does compost help growing plants?

For this activity you will need:

* 4 small plant pots (about as big as your fist)
* Potting soil
* Worm compost
* Measuring jug
* Bean seeds
* Water
* Tape for labelling pots
* Marker
* A ruler
* A notebook

6 Check your plants each day to see when the seeds sprout. For each pot, record the date when the seeds begin to grow.

7 After the plants sprout, observe their growth. Every two days, measure the height of the taller plant in each pot with a ruler. Record the height of the taller plant in each pot.

8 Count the number of leaves that each plant grows. Record the number of leaves for each pot.

9 Your pots may become crowded as the plants grow. Weed out the shorter plant in each pot. Keep the taller plant in each pot.

10 Continue to record the height of the plants and the number of leaves. As flowers begin to grow, count and record the number of flowers on each plant.

	POT A	POT B	POT C	POT D
Date				
Number of plants growing				
Height				
Number of leaves				
Number of flowers				

Does adding worm compost to soil make bean plants grow taller?

Helping plants grow

Which bean plants grew the best in your experiment? You probably found that adding compost helped your plants to sprout and grow. Adding 45 ml (3 tablespoons) of compost in a pot might have helped a plant grow taller and grow more leaves than adding 15 ml (1 tablespoon) of compost.

But you might have found that you can add too much compost to the soil. Growing plants in half worm compost and half soil probably did not help the plants grow more, and may even have harmed them. Compost helps plants to grow, but too much compost can slow down their growth.

Compost makes soil fertile

Why does compost help plants? Compost is rich in **nutrients**. Nutrients are like vitamin pills for plants. Plants need them to grow healthy and strong. Many of the nutrients that were in the vegetable scraps you fed your worms ended up in worm compost. Without enough nutrients, plant growth is slower.

When worms eat their way through soil, they take in **bacteria** and other microscopic **decomposers**. Many of these decomposers are still alive after travelling through a worm's digestive tract. The bacteria that a worm does not **digest** are mixed in with worm casts. Bacteria and other decomposers help break down the dead **matter** in the soil and improve it.

Worm slime

When worms digest their food, it gets mixed with slimy **mucus**. Some of the mucus travels through a worm and comes out in its casts. The mucus in worm compost also helps plants grow. Nutrients stick to the mucus and are not washed away.

Because of the mucus in worm casts, soil mixed with worm compost holds more water. The soil dries out less often, and the plants absorb more water through their roots. With more nutrients and water, plants grow faster. They grow larger roots and stems and also more leaves. They can make more flowers and fruits.

When worm compost is mixed with soil, plants can grow better.

Worms and soil

Tunnelling through soil
For this activity you will need:

* A glass jar (litre or quart size)
* Plastic wrap
* Soil
* Sand
* Crumpled dead leaves
* A pencil
* Worms (either red worms from a worm farm or earthworms from the ground)

Steps to follow

 1 Set up a jar to watch worms tunnel through soil. Place a layer of damp soil in the bottom of the jar, about 2.5 cm (1 inch) thick.

 2 Cover the soil with a layer of damp sand, about 2.5 cm (1 inch) thick.

 3 Continue adding layers of soil and sand until the jar is nearly full.

 4 Place three to five worms on the top layer. Crumple up a couple of dead leaves and put them over the worms.

 5 Cover the top of the jar with plastic wrap. Punch a couple of small holes in the wrap with a pencil. This will allow air into your jar.

6 Put the jar in a cupboard or other dark place.

 7 Check your jar in three days, and again at the end of a week. How far have the worms tunnelled down? Where are the dead leaves? Have the layers of sand and soil changed? Look for open spaces and note where you see them. When you are finished with your observations, return the worms and soil to the ground outside.

Tunnels help plants

Worm tunnels improve soil for plant growth. When worms tunnel, they make openings that can fill with air and water. Air can move further down in worm tunnels, allowing **decomposers** to survive there. Plant roots can grow into these spaces, too.

Worms mix up the soil. They take leaves from the surface and bring them underground. There, **bacteria**, **moulds**, and other decomposers can feed on and break down dead plants. Worms also bring up **minerals** from deeper in the soil to the surface.

Tunnels hold water

A field with worm tunnels can soak up 4 to 10 times more rainwater than one without tunnels.

Tunnelling worms improve the soil by making spaces for air and water.

Steps to follow

1 Some soils are better for growing plants than others. Dig up soil from two different locations. Choose one place with bare ground or with sandy soil. Choose another place with dark-coloured soil, such as a vegetable garden. From each site, dig up a clump of soil about the size of your fist. Put each soil sample in a separate plastic bag.

2 From your worm farm, dig up a similar-sized clump of worm **compost**. Choose a clump of compost that is broken down, without pieces of bedding or food scraps.

3 Fill each jar with water, to about 2.5 cm (1 inch) from the top.

4 Put one soil or compost sample in each mesh bag.

5 Slowly lower the soils down into the water, and watch closely. Which samples fall apart in the water? Which samples stay clumped together?

Soil structure

For this activity you will need:

* 3 wide-mouth glass jars
* 3 plastic mesh bags (from onions or oranges). 0.5 cm (1/4 inch) mesh holes work best
* Soil samples
* Water
* 3 plastic bags (sandwich size or larger)

Compost makes soils stick

Soil with a lot of compost in it stays clumped together, even when put in water. During a rainstorm, soils with compost do not wash away. The **decayed** plant **matter** makes the soil stick together. Soils with compost will hold water. The nutrients in the soil stick to the soil particles and do not wash away.

Soils with compost hold more water and nutrients, so plants grow better.

Sand washes away

Sandy soils fall apart in water. During a rainstorm, water washes away sandy soils. The sandy soils cannot store water or hold many **nutrients**. Plants have a harder time growing because sandy soils dry up and do not have many nutrients.

Gardeners and farmers often add compost to sandy soils. That improves the soils so that they can hold more water, air, and nutrients. Plants can then grow better in them.

Composting helps the Earth

By starting a worm farm and changing your food scraps into **compost**, you help the Earth. Instead of throwing away your leftovers, you can turn them into compost. Instead of making more waste, you can make healthy soil that helps plants grow.

In a landfill

What happens to food waste if you do not compost it? A rubbish truck probably takes your food waste to a **landfill**. Landfills are not made to help waste break down. They are designed to store waste. Landfills have clay or plastic liners on the sides and the bottom. This keeps chemicals from seeping out into soil or water. Since air is not mixed into the rubbish in landfills, few **decomposers** can live there. One scientist dug up food wastes from a landfill. He found that 30 years later, the food scraps had still not decomposed at all.

When a landfill is full, workers cover it with clay and soil. The rubbish remains buried there. Because most people do not want to live near a landfill, communities have trouble finding a place for rubbish after a landfill is full.

Reducing waste

By using a worm farm, you send less rubbish to a landfill. That means that there will be less need for new landfills in the future. How much less food waste do you make because of a worm farm? If you feed your worms 1.6 kg (3.5 pounds) of food scraps a week, then you will send 78 kg (182 pounds) less waste to a landfill each year.

How else can you reduce your food waste?

- You can make an outdoor compost pile for your garden waste.
- You can reuse and **recycle** containers instead of throwing them out.
- Try packing a lunch for school that will not make any waste for the bin.
- Feed your leftovers to the worms!

When worms eat your leftovers,
you send less waste to a landfill.

Glossary

anus opening at the lower end of the digestive tract through which waste exits. Worm casts go out through the anus.

bacteria tiny one-celled life-form

blood vessel tube through which the blood circulates. Blood vessels bring energy and oxygen to each segment of a worm.

bristle stiff, hair-like structure that a worm uses for crawling. A worm pushes its bristles against the ground.

cast worm faeces. Worm casts contain soil, bacteria, and plant matter.

clitellum swollen band on a worm that makes cocoons with eggs inside. More than one are called clitella.

cocoon protective case that contains eggs. A worm cocoon usually has one to five babies inside.

compost mixture of decayed matter that can be used to help plants grow. When you compost food scraps, you recycle them.

consumer organism that feeds on other organisms. You are a consumer because you eat plants and animals.

decay break down into smaller parts; to rot. Worms decay leaves when they break them down into tiny pieces.

decomposer organism that breaks down dead plants or animals. Bacteria, fungi, and worms are decomposers.

digest convert food into simple chemicals that the body can use. The material that a worm does not digest comes out as worm casts.

dissolve become part of a liquid. Worms breathe oxygen that dissolves in the liquid next to their skin.

energy source of power. Fossil fuel, electricity, and solar power are different kinds of energy.

fertile rich material that helps plants grow. Adding compost to soil makes the soil more fertile.

fertilize when a sperm joins with an egg to make a new individual. A worm's eggs are fertilized in its clitellum.

fertilizer substance added to soil to help plants grow

food chain sequence of plants and animals, showing the flow of energy as food from one to the next. The flow of energy from grass to a cow to a person can be shown in a food chain.

food web series of linked food chains. Owls, foxes, mice, and rabbits are all part of a meadow food web.

fruiting body part of a fungus that makes spores. Mushrooms are fruiting bodies.

fungus (plural: **fungi**) organism that absorbs its food from dead matter. Unlike plants, fungi cannot make their own food.

gizzard part of the digestive tract with thick muscles that grinds food particles. A worm's food is ground up in its gizzard.

habitat area where a community of plants and animals live. Worms are important animals in the soil habitat.

hermaphrodite organism that has both male and female parts. Worms are hermaphrodites.

intestine tube where food is digested. After food is ground up in a worm's gizzard, it goes into the intestine.

landfill large outdoor area used for waste disposal. The rubbish that you throw away is taken to a landfill.

matter physical substance. Decomposers break down the matter in plants and animals.

mineral solid chemical substance found in Earth's surface – for example, quartz or crystal

mould type of fungi. Moulds can grow on bread and other food.

mucus slimy substance that helps food pass through the intestines. Some of a worm's mucus comes out with its casts.

nerve fibre that passes messages around a body. Earthworms have nerves in each segment of the body.

nutrient chemical needed by plants and animals for growing and living. Nitrogen and phosphorous are nutrients.

producer green plant or other organism that can make its own food. Trees and grass are producers.

recycle take unwanted material and make something useful out of it

reproduce make a new individual. Earthworms can reproduce in a worm farm.

segment one part of an organism. Earthworms have 100 or more segments.

sperm male reproductive cell. After a sperm joins with an egg, the egg can grow into a new individual.

spore single cell that can grow into a new individual. When a mould spore lands on a piece of bread, it starts to grow.

Find out more

Books

Does an Earthworm Have a Girlfriend? Anna Claybourne
(Raintree 2005)

This book explains how an earthworm reproduces.

Food Chains and Webs: From Producers to Decomposers, Louise
and Richard Spilsbury (Heinemann Library, 2005)

This book explores the producers and decomposers in food chains, using
examples from everyday life.

Minibeasts on a Compost Heap, Sarah Ridley
(Franklin Watts, 2008)

This book investigates how small animals live, grow, and interact with
their environment.

Websites

Create less waste

www.lovefoodhatewaste.com/

Find out why cutting food waste matters and what you can do about it.

Recycle now!

www.recyclenow.com/fun_stuff/index.html

Watch a video about recycling and learn what happens in your compost bin.

Recycle zone

www.recyclezone.org.uk/az_worms.aspx

Learn all about worms, inside and out. Find out fun facts about worms.

Organization

The Soil Association
South Plaza
Marlborough Street
Bristol, BS1 3NX

www.soilassociation.org

This environmental charity promotes organic farming and has information on composting and worm farms.

Place to visit

The Eden Project
Bodelva
St Austell
Cornwall
PL24 2SG
www.edenproject.com

Index